# DANNY
# BOY

. . .

# DANNY BOY

## The Beloved Irish Ballad

by

## MALACHY McCOURT

RUNNING PRESS

PHILADELPHIA • LONDON

9   8   7   6   5   4   3
Digit on the right indicates the number of this printing

Library of Congress Cataloging-in-Publication Number 2001087045

ISBN 0-7624-1124-4

Acquired by Danielle McCole
Interior designed by Bill Jones
Edited by Hamilton Cain, Gilbert King, and Molly Jay
Typography: Centaur

This book may be ordered by mail from the publisher. Please include
$2.50 for postage and handling.
**But try your bookstore first!**

Running Press Book Publishers
125 South Twenty-second Street
Philadelphia, Pennsylvania 19103-4399

Visit us on the web!
www.runningpress.com

$W$ith awe and profound respect
I dedicate this small tome to the
Bravest and the Finest—
the firefighters and police officers
of New York City—
who went through Hell
on their way to Heaven
at about 9 a.m.
on the 11th of September, 2001.

# ACKNOWLEDGMENTS

With thanks to my young pal and collaborator, Danielle McCole (Danny Girl), without whose help "Danny Boy" would still be reposing in my mind.

To Seamus Heaney, Nobel Laureate, who took time to share his thoughts. To my brother, Frank. To my friends Judy Collins, Roma Downey, Hector Elizondo, Liam Neeson, Gabriel Byrne, Larry Kirwan of Black 47, and Martin Sheen for time, thoughts, and words.

To Michael Robinson and his Standing Stones Web site (www.standingstones.com) for the fantastic amount of information on the history of "Danny Boy."

To the dioceses of Providence and the Archdioceses of Boston and New York for prohibiting the singing of "Danny Boy" at funeral masses.

To the amazing Mick Maloney for the quiet writing haven and for his inspiration.

To my editor Molly Jay who exercised great patience and forbearance as I missed several deadlines.

And to Diana, my greatest friend and spouse, for all the encouragement.

# TABLE OF CONTENTS

*Introduction*                                                      10

*An Ave there for me*
The Melody                                                          14

*From glen to glen*
Lyrics Meet Melody                                                  32

*The pipes are calling*
The Questions                                                       52

*The valley's hushed and white with snow*
The Land of Derry                                                   72

*Tell me that you love me*
The Pop History of "Danny Boy"                                      88

*Epilogue*
*In sunshine or in shadow*
What Does It All mean?                                              96

*Appendix*
Discography and Timeline                                           106

# INTRODUCTION

Anyone who has ever claimed Irish roots or been within earshot of a pub on the 17th of March has, knowingly or not, catalogued the tune of "Danny Boy" in the music box of their memory. The mystery and myth surrounding the air has elevated it from beloved ballad to sacred script. As if passed from generation to generation through a game of "whispering down the lane," where one child whispers a story into the ear of another, and the story transforms along a chain of children, the story of this song has metamorphosed.

Officially, "Danny Boy" is a song of two verses totaling 155 words. Speculation about the meaning of these words is as ripe as when the song was first published in 1913, a year before World War I broke out in Europe. While the lyricist is known to us, the composer's name is still uncertain. Here, then, I have tried to throw the requisite light on the melody's murky origins so that all singers can raise their voices with fervor or in sorrow or with passion, and attain a deeper understanding of the song that has inspired so much emotion for generations.

It is generally assumed that "Danny Boy" is an Irish song, but most people will be surprised to learn that whilst the air is sprung from Hibernian roots, a biddable British barrister by the name of Fred may well have penned the words while riding to court on a commuter train. A great many questions have been raised regarding the nuances and connotations of the song. "Danny Boy" speaks to Irish society, politics, religion, war, economics, sports, and, of course, the history of Irish art and music, a song that encompasses and encourages intense nationalistic pride. In these pages we'll go back to the Land of Derry, where legend says the tune to our boy Danny was born, and along the way, we'll attempt to uncover two of the biggest uncertainties surrounding "Danny Boy": The origin of the melody (known as the Derry air or the Londonderry air) and exactly who is addressing Danny in the song.

From a performance perspective, it's understandable how John McDermott and Rosemary Clooney might have been inspired to add "Danny Boy" to their repertoires, but we'll also discover how latter day crooners such as Eric Clapton and the late Freddie Mercury could not resist the call of the pipes. Ballad singers, wedding singers, pub singers, opera singers, pop singers and even non-singers continue to reprise this song, because the sentiments affect the heart and the music of it has endured for three hundred years, making it one of the greatest perennials of all time.

Oh, Danny boy, the pipes,
the pipes are calling

From glen to glen and down
the mountain side

The summer's gone
and all the flowers are dying

'Tis you, 'tis you must go
and I must bide.


But come ye back
when summer's in the meadow

Or when the valley's hushed
and white with snow

'Tis I'll be here in sunshine
or in shadow

Oh, Danny boy, oh Danny boy, I love
you so!

And if ye come,
and all the flow'rs are dying

If I am dead, as dead
I well may be,

Ye'll come and find the place
where I am lying

And kneel and say an Ave there
for me.


And I shall hear, though soft you tread
above me,

And all my grave will warmer,
sweeter be,

For you will bend and tell me that
you love me,

And I shall sleep in peace
until you come to me.

—*Frederick Edward Weatherly*

An
Ave
there
for
me

# The Melody

$\mathcal{T}$here's an odd bunch roaming this earth, generally known as collectors. They purchase, exchange, swap, and steal all manner of material goods: stamps, pottery, paintings, baseball cards, furniture, and coins; they even stockpile and trade items like Coca Cola bottles and old shoes. The oddest of the lot might actually be the folk song singer, almost always collectors as well as performers. It is not at all unusual for the singer to offer a long peroration about a particular song he or she is about to sing. The peroration usually follows the same literary path as romantic fiction, and typically, the singer will emerge as hero and preserver of some ancient culture. Surely you've seen it before. The spotlight dims and the folksinger pauses to introduce the next song with all the ham-handed subtlety of a Las Vegas magician. It might go something like this:

THIS NEXT SONG HAS A LITTLE STORY TO IT.
(PAUSE, LONG SIP FROM PINT GLASS). I HAPPENED
TO BE DRIVING ONE STORMY NIGHT IN THE
WILDEST PART OF THE MOUNTAINS OF DONEGAL,
THE OUTER HEBRIDES, OR IN THE MOST RURAL
PART OF APPALACHIA, WHEN MY CAR ENGINE
SUDDENLY, WITHOUT ANY REASON, STALLED ON
THIS DARK, DESERTED, COUNTRY ROAD. I CHECKED
THE GAS AND THERE WAS PLENTY AND I TRIED TO
START IT AGAIN, BUT HAD NO SUCCESS. SITTING
THERE IN THE SILENT DARKNESS WAS QUITE SCARY
AND SO I DECIDED TO WALK TO THE NEAREST
HOUSE. IT BEGAN TO RAIN HEAVILY AND THE WIND
MADE IT DIFFICULT TO WALK, BUT I TUCKED MY
HEAD DOWN AND MOVED ON. AFTER ABOUT AN
HOUR, I SPIED A LIGHT WHICH SEEMED TO BE
HANGING IN THE SKY, AS IT WAS ON THE SIDE OF A
MOUNTAIN, AND I DECIDED TO HEAD IN THAT
DIRECTION. THE GOING WAS TREACHEROUS, MUDDY,
AND SLIPPERY, BUT I STRUGGLED ON, SURE TO MAIN-
TAIN A VIEW OF THE LIGHT. JUST WHEN I THOUGHT
I COULDN'T WALK ANY FURTHER, I HEARD THE
MOST BEAUTIFUL SOUND, A HUMAN VOICE RAISED IN

SONG AND ACCOMPANIED BY THE UNDERTONES OF A
VIOLIN. IT WAS A MAN'S VOICE AND THE WORDS
WERE CLEAR, AND I COULD UNDERSTAND THEM
EVEN WITH THE SOUNDS OF WIND AND RAIN
WHIPPING AROUND ME. HE SANG OF THE LOSS OF
HIS LOVE AND OF THE BREAKING OF HIS HEART
BECAUSE SHE HAD CHOSEN ANOTHER. THERE WAS A
GREAT SOB IN HIS THROAT AND WHEN THE PAIN
BECAME TOO GREAT, THE WAIL OF THE VIOLIN PLED
FOR HER RETURN AND THEN THERE WAS SILENCE.
GATHERING MY WITS, I KNOCKED ON THE DOOR
AND A VOICE BADE ME "COME IN." IT WAS A SHABBY
PLACE WITH HAND-CRAFTED WOOD FURNITURE, A
TABLE AND A COUPLE OF BENCHES, BUT IT WAS
WARM. A VOICE SAID, "YOU ARE WELCOME IN MY
HOUSE." IT WAS THE VOICE OF AN OLD MAN
SEATED IN A ROCKING CHAIR BESIDE A COMFORTABLE
FIRE. HE HAD A VERY SUSPICIOUS DOG, WITH HEAD
ALERT, SEATED BESIDE HIM. I REALIZED THAT THE
MAN WAS TOTALLY BLIND. I EXPLAINED THAT I WAS
A TRAVELING MUSICIAN STRANDED ON THE ROAD
AND NEEDED SHELTER FOR THE NIGHT. THAT
PRESENTED NO PROBLEM TO HIM, AS HE SAID HE
HAD PLENTY OF ROOM. HE OFFERED ME FOOD AND

DRINK AND TALK OF MUSIC AND OF SONG. HE TOLD
ME THE SONG THAT I HAD HEARD OUTSIDE HAD
BEEN THE STORY OF HIS ANCESTOR TWO HUNDRED
YEARS BEFORE AND HAD BEEN HANDED DOWN FROM
GENERATION TO GENERATION. I ASKED HIM FOR THE
WORDS AND I MANAGED TO ANNOTATE THE MUSIC
AND (WIPING A TEAR) THIS IS THE SONG YOU ARE
ABOUT TO HEAR.

The common feature that all of these collectors of song stories share is the presence of a warm-hearted blind fiddler. The implication, of course, is that blindness confers a special power on a human, an extraordinary insight (yes, insight) into the soul or, at the very least, a sharp ear for bad music. Whatever the reason, the world has no shortage of collector/folk singers who have experienced some kind of spiritual adventure with blind fiddlers who live in remote areas of the world, unspoiled by technology. Just once I'd like to hear the story end with the folk singer returning to the fiddler's cabin with a royalty check.

The poet Yeats was fascinated by the spiritual force of blindness, as he wrote of Blind Raftery's (also a poet and a fiddler) hold over the imaginations of men:

*I am Raftery the poet*
*Full of hope and love*
*My eyes without sight*
*My mind without torment*
*Going west on my journey*
*By the light of my heart*
*Tired and weary*
*To the end of the road*
*Behold me now*
*With my back to the wall*
*Playing music*
*To empty pockets*

—From *1000 Years of Irish Poetry*
from Welcome Rain Press

I don't know how many blind fiddlers ambled about
Ireland, but they clearly monopolized wisdom and old
tunes. The story behind the discovery of the Derry air, the
Londonderry air if you wish, is sadly, not much of an
exception. Legend has it that a blind fiddler may have
unwittingly channeled this song to us through an alert
Anglo Saxon woman named Jane Ross. But more on Miss
Ross in a moment.

Some evidence suggests that the Londonderry air was composed by one Rory Dall O'Cahan, (1660-1712) an Irish harpist who wandered about Scotland going by the name of Rory Dall Morrison, and eventually became known simply as Rory Dall. Traveling pipers and fiddlers sitting in on sessions and joining in the various *feiseanna* (musical gatherings) influenced each other musically, thus tracing the exact composer of a centuries-old Irish or Scottish melody is no easy task for even the most determined music scholars.

We can thank Dr. George Petrie who published the melody in 1855 in Ancient Music of Ireland. Petrie, an enthusiastic aficionado of Irish music gives full credit to Miss Jane Ross of Limavady, County Derry, for placing the piece at his disposal. Ross, educated in music and an avid collector of things musically Irish, claimed to have taken the tune down after hearing it played by an itinerant piper. According to Petrie:

FOR THE FOLLOWING BEAUTIFUL AIR I HAVE TO EXPRESS MY VERY GRATEFUL ACKNOWLEDGEMENT OF MISS J. ROSS, OF LIMAVADY, IN THE COUNTY OF LONDONDERRY, A LADY WHO HAS MADE A LARGE COLLECTION OF THE POPULAR UNPUBLISHED

MELODIES OF THAT COUNTY, WHICH SHE HAS VERY
KINDLY PLACED AT MY DISPOSAL, AND WHICH HAS
ADDED VERY CONSIDERABLY TO THE STOCK OF TUNES
WHICH I HAD PREVIOUSLY ACQUIRED FROM THAT
STILL VERY IRISH COUNTY. I SAY STILL VERY IRISH:
FOR THOUGH IT HAS BEEN PLANTED FOR MORE
THAN TWO CENTURIES BY ENGLISH AND SCOTTISH
SETTLERS, THE OLD IRISH RACE STILL FORMS THE
GREAT MAJORITY OF ITS PEASANT INHABITANTS; AND
THERE ARE FEW, IF ANY, COUNTIES IN WHICH, WITH
LESS FOREIGN ADMIXTURE, THE ANCIENT MELODIES
OF THE COUNTRY HAVE BEEN SO EXTENSIVELY PRE-
SERVED. THE NAME OF THE TUNE UNFORTUNATELY
WAS NOT ASCERTAINED BY MISS ROSS, WHO SENT IT
TO ME WITH THE SIMPLE REMARK THAT IT WAS "VERY
OLD," IN THE CORRECTNESS OF WHICH STATEMENT
I HAVE NO HESITATION IN EXPRESSING MY PERFECT
CONCURRENCE.

Miss Jane Ross left no record of the name of the piper,
nor the type of pipes she saw and heard, but archivists and
cultural detectives have been able to piece together some
clues. Miss Ross was allegedly a composer herself, as all
collectors must be, but there is no clear evidence of her

work. However, there is a McCurry family of Ireland that has claimed that an ancestor by the name of Jimmy McCurry was a blind fiddler (not a piper) who played at the fairs at Limavady around the same time Ross lived in that village. On Fair Day many farmers came to town to sell their cattle, sheep, pigs, and chickens, and their wives would often trade knitwear, eggs, and butter, as well as shop for household staples. Their commercial activity then drew all manner of entertainers, such as card sharks, tumblers, singers, fortune tellers, matchmakers, and the like. There was always great excitement on these days, and the assembled musicians garnered enough in offerings to last for several months, if they spent wisely. Of course, drinking was abundant; fights would often break out, with people walloping each other with blackthorn sticks, cudgels and shillaleaghs, a weapon harder than most farmers' heads. When that activity grew tedious, the participants cleaned up the blood, brushed themselves off and drank to each other's health. "Slainte Agus Saol Agat," meaning "health and wealth to you", they would say, and carry on with song and music. A young man named Matt Talbot, a notorious drunk, would do anything to satisfy his craving, and one day he stole the fiddle of a blind man and pawned it for drink. After he sobered up, Matt felt a twinge of guilt and sought to make amends by securing a new instrument for the fiddler. Despite an extensive search, he never found the man again, and to the day he died on June 7th, 1925, he regretted his awful deed. Because of his lifelong commitment toward sobriety and clean living, Talbot has since been venerated by Pope Paul VI in 1975 and is a second stage candidate for sainthood in the Catholic church. If confirmed, he will become the patron saint of alcoholics. So there is forgiveness.

One thing we do know is that Talbot was born five years after Jane Ross heard the music of the Londonderry air, so it's not likely that both he and Ross had historic encounters with the same blind fiddler. However, the story of Jimmy McCurry, the man many believe is "the blind fiddler" Ross reputedly heard, is told in the book *The Blind Fiddler from Myroe* by Jim Hunter (University of Ulster, 1997). The work excerpted below is just a small part of Jimmy's story:

THE LIMAVADY MARKET WAS A FAVOURITE DESTINA-
TION FOR JIMMY. ALL THE FARMERS USED TO BRING
THEIR HORSES AND CARTS TO MAINE STREET. AFTER
THEY HAD UNYOKED THEIR HORSES THEY LEFT
THEIR CARTS WITH SHAFTS ON THE GROUND ALL

LINED UP ALONG THE STREET. JIMMY TOOK UP
POSITION BETWEEN THE SHAFTS WITH HIS FIDDLE AT
HIS FAVOURITE SPOT OUTSIDE BURNS AND LAIRDS
SHIPPING LINE OFFICE. INTERESTINGLY, THIS OFFICE
WAS JUST OPPOSITE THE HOME OF JANE ROSS, WHO
ANNOTATED THE MUSIC OF THE "LONDONDERRY
AIR" FROM AN ITINERANT FIDDLER IN 1851.

Some oral evidence suggests that Jimmy was the "itinerant
fiddler." Wallace McCurry tells a story related to him by
his grandfather, a contemporary of the blind fiddler:

ONE DAY JANE HEARD JIMMY PLAYING A BEAUTIFUL
MELODY OUTSIDE THE SHIPPING LINE OFFICE WHICH
SHE HAD NEVER HEARD BEFORE. SHE CAME ACROSS
AND ASKED HIM TO PLAY IT AGAIN TO ENABLE HER TO
NOTE DOWN THE TUNE. JANE THANKED HIM AND
GAVE HIM A COIN FOR HIS MOVING RENDITION OF
THE TUNE. WHEN SHE DEPARTED HE RUBBED IT
AGAINST HIS LIPS, AS WAS HIS CUSTOM, AND DISCOV-
ERED IT WAS A FLORIN AND NOT THE CUSTOMARY
PENNY. HE SET OFF IN PURSUIT AND WHEN HE
CAUGHT UP WITH HER HE TOLD HER THAT SHE HAD
MADE A MISTAKE. JANE REFUSED TO TAKE IT BACK AND

ASKED HIM TO KEEP IT AS A TOKEN OF HER APPRECI-
ATION FOR HIS MUSIC.

Jimmy may have also produced lyrics for the melody. "I
have discovered no less than six different sets of lyrics to
accompany the Londonderry air," said Margaret Cowan,
ranger at the Roe Valley Country Park. "It is just possible
that one of these is the work of the blind fiddler from
Myroe." [pp. 9-10]

As recounted here, Jimmy would have been in his
early twenties if and when he met Miss Jane Ross, and
although he was well known, both as a colorful character
and as a fiddler, she did not mention his name or the name
of any other fiddler or piper. With some of the British
upper classes, it was a point of pride not to know the
names of social inferiors. Such knowledge would have
indicated a degree of familiarity deemed unacceptable in
that social stratum. It may have been that Miss Ross failed
to identify McCurry by name for this reason.

Jimmy McCurry, however, is not credited with any
lyrics to the Londonderry air. Some music historians have
noted that there were many versions of lyrics written for
the air prior to the turn of the twentieth century. Most of
them were written after Petrie published the melody in

1855. According to *The Fireside Book of Folk Songs*, the following words were the first ever set to the Londonderry air:

*Would God I were the tender apple blossom*
*That floats and falls from off the twisted bough*
*To lie and faint within your silken bosom*
*Within your silken bosom as that does now.*
*Or would I were a little burnish'd apple*
*For you to pluck me, gliding by so cold*
*While sun and shade you robe of lawn will dapple*
*Your robe of lawn, and you hair's spun gold.*

*Yea, would to God I were among the roses*
*That lean to kiss you as you float between*
*While on the lowest branch a bud uncloses*
*A bud uncloses, to touch you, queen.*
*Nay, since you will not love, would I were growing*
*A happy daisy, in the garden path*
*That so your silver foot might press me going*
*Might press me going even unto death.*

It's interesting to note that the air has often inspired themes of death and farewells. Thomas Moore (1770-1852) wrote a ten-volume work, *Irish Melodies* (1807-

1834), consisting of 130 poems set to music with the help of Sir John Stevenson. One of the poems, "My Gentle Harp," is another early precursor to "Danny Boy":

*My gentle harp, once more I waken*
*The sweetness of thy slumb'ring strain*
*In tears our last farewell was taken*
*And now in tears we meet again.*
*Yet even then, while peace was singing,*
*Her halcyon song o'er land and sea,*
*Though joy and hope to others bringing,*
*She only brought new tears to thee.*
*Then who can ask for notes of pleasure,*
*My drooping harp, from chords like thine?*
*Alas, the lark's gay morning measure*
*As ill would suit the swan's decline.*
*Or how shall I, who love, who bless thee,*
*Invoke thy breath for freedom's strains,*
*When e'en the wreaths in which I dress thee,*
*Are sadly mixed, half flours, half chains.*

But before Moore and even the Londonderry air itself, a melody strikingly similar to "Danny Boy" was published in James *Irish Minstrels*, in 1831. The song, "Aisling an

Agfhir" or "The Young Man's Dream" had English words
in addition to accompanying Gaelic text. It's a song that,
on the surface, tells of a young man's love for a beautiful
woman in lament. Upon closer inspection, of "The
Young Man's Dream", however, the woman is clearly
Ireland, a forerunner of the "Caitlin/Kathleen" songs,
with themes of nature, loyalty and sacrifice.

*In a dream of delusion, methought I was laid,*
*By a brook overarched with a fluttering shade;*
*A delicious recess, where silver-tongued rills,*
*And far cataracts deep roar echoed round from the hills;*
*Gleaming fish in clear waters were wantonly playing,*
*And hoarse murmuring bees o'er wild flow'rets were straying;*
*While sweet honey distilled from old oaks to regale,*
*The young and the fair in that odorous vale.*


*A beautiful bird on a blossomy spray,*
*Was warbling a varied and rapturous lay;*
*As I listened entranced in delightful surprise,*
*A lovely enchantress astonished my eye;*
*Her cheeks like the quicken's rich clusters were glowing,*
*Her amber silk locks to her white ancles flowing;*
*Like a keen freezing star gleamed each sparkling blue eye,*

Alas! in one month, for her loss, I must die.

When first she descried me, startled, alarmed,
And with coy supplication my sympathy charmed:
Oh favoured of men! do not ruin a maid,
By fate to your power unprotected betrayed;
For with sorrow and shame broken hearted I'd die,
Or for life thro' wild desarts a lunatic fly.

Oh peerless perfection! how canst thou believe,
That I could such innocence hurt or deceive?
I implore the Great Fountain of glory and love,
And all the blessed saints in their synod above;
That connubial affections our souls may combine,
And the pearl of her sex be immutably mine.
The green grass shall not grow, nor the sun shed his light,
Nor the fair moon and stars gem the forehead of night;
The stream shall flow upward, the fish quit the sea,
Ere I shall prove faithless, dear angel to thee.
Her ripe lip and soft bosom then gently I prest,
And clasped her half-blushing consent to my breast;
My heart fluttered light as a bird on the spray,
But I woke, and alas, the vain dream fled away.

There is more evidence of late, this time in the form of

an ancient Scottish manuscript, which dates the melody as far back as the early 1700s. It may well be that the tune originated, or was at least annotated in Lowland Scotland, and it may well be that the melody was simply well-traveled and retooled from region to region. In short, there is no telling when or where the melody truly originated. Historians can only rely on written records, and, as you can see, even these are open to speculation and unverifiable conjecture. The air's conception, hardly immaculate, may be the one mystery of "Danny Boy" that can truly never be solved. But despair not. Let us move on now to the other great mystery!

# From glen to glen

# Lyrics Meet
# Melody

Whether or not the tune, air or melody we now know as "Danny Boy" was composed in Ireland some three hundred years ago, there is no doubt about the origin of the words. The lyrics are not Irish and they were not written by an Irishman, and no matter how vehemently the Irish claim authorship to the song, the fact remains that "Danny Boy" was written by, of all people, a British lawyer. After countless attempts by others, such as Alfred Perceval Graves and Edward Lawson, who put words to the Londonderry air, the ones that finally took root were those of an Englishman who probably never set foot in Ireland, and pulled the "Danny Boy" lyrics out of a dead file of his own failed songs. He could never have realized the impact his words would have on future generations whose eyes would well up with tears before the first line of the song was finished. And he might have been equally surprised by the amount of intrigue and mystery surrounding the words he wrote.

Indeed, an English barrister by the name of Frederick Edward Weatherly put pen to paper and gave birth to the boy Danny. The son of a country doctor, Weatherly was born one of thirteen children in 1848 in Portishead, England, a small fishing village in Somerset on the shore of the Bristol Channel. While his childhood was certainly not one of privilege, he grew up in an artistic and intellectual environment, discovering the pleasures of the classic poets at an early age.

Weatherly also had early recollections of his mother's fondness for folk songs from England, Wales, Scotland, and Ireland. In *Piano and Gown*, (G.P. Putnam's Sons, 1926) the autobiography he penned in his seventies, Weatherly recalled specific melodies his mother sung around the house, and he credited her voice as a kind of muse for his songwriting, even into the latter stages of his songwriting career. In fact, Fred's mother may well be the answer to one of the song's mysteries.

In 1859, Weatherly attended the Hereford Cathedral School where his exposure to art and music took hold. "It was the music of the place for which my thanksgiving is the deepest," he wrote in *Piano and Gown*. He became so fascinated with the performances of the cathedral choir that "if I could squeeze in half an hour between football and tea I did so." In spite of his passion for romance and poetry and song, Weatherly did not write verses himself until the end of his schooldays, "when I burst into song in the shape of two exceedingly doleful elegies, one in English and one in Latin," on the death of a Dean at the school. This marked a poignant turning moment in his life, since it was the first time he felt comfortable expressing himself in such a manner. In 1867, Weatherly was awarded a scholarship to Oxford, and at the age of eighteen, he left his small-town life for good.

"I went to Oxford with my visions limited," he wrote, "my knowledge and range of literature circumscribed. The poets I loved were Byron, Tennyson, Longfellow and James Thomson, the Thomson who wrote "The Seasons." And when I began my life at Oxford, I found myself among books and pictures and men of whom in my little world at school I had only faintly heard."

He proved to be a mediocre student at Oxford. The College Musical Society became a "charming distraction" to his studies, and later, the Oxford University Dramatic Society captivated his interests. He inscribed his first "words for music" for his friend Joseph Roeckel in 1868. Roeckel taught him the musical requirements of song, and the next two lyrics he penned were for Molloy and Michael Maybrick (who worked under the pseudonym of Stephen Adams). Weatherly described these two composers as his "first, best and dearest in the world of music." He later credited Molloy, a poet, as the man who taught him his trade. Weatherly felt he owed Molloy a great debt of gratitude for suggesting subjects for lyrics, as well as helping him to improve them, and the two collaborated on several songs.

On a more sensational note, the Maybrick name was a familiar one to British newspapers in 1889. James Maybrick, Molloy's brother, was poisoned to death and the main suspect was James' young American wife, Florie, who eventually stood trial, was convicted, and sentenced to fifteen years in prison. The murder trial was covered extensively in the British press and considered by many pundits and legalists to have been a miscarriage of justice. Florie's conviction actually led to significant reforms in the British legal system. Over a hundred years later, conspiracy theorists began mentioning James Maybrick as a possible suspect in the Jack the Ripper murders because of the dubious discovery of a diary, "found" in the early 1990s, purported to belong to James. The diary was later assumed by "Ripperologists" to be a hoax, but not before more adventurous conspiracy buffs tried to link poor

Fred, because of his legal position and relationship with the Maybricks, into the tangled web of the Jack the Ripper murders. It's my opinion that Weatherly's prolific songwriting career, (estimated at 3,000 songs) in addition to his full time work as a barrister, left him little time or energy to be traipsing about London in the wee hours with cloak and dagger. So let's relegate Fred to only the mysteries of "Danny Boy."

In 1873, Weatherly married, finished his schooling at Oxford, and set about to coach pupils in subjects such as Greek and English. He also spent much of his free time penning lyrics. He wrote for *Life*, the *Whitehall Review*, *London Society*, and *Cassell's Magazine*, as well as books for children and some verses for Christmas cards. "But not mottoes for crackers," he wrote, bursting with pride. "I drew the line there."

Weatherly songs have been enjoyed by millions all over the English speaking world, yet he was quite modest in his praise for himself. He allocated most of the credit to the musicians and singers who spread his words to the hearts of the people. "I do not claim to be a 'poet,'" he wrote in *Piano and Gown*. "I don't pretend that my songs are 'literary,' but they are 'songs of the people' and that is enough for me."

As Weatherly began his career, the influence of his mother and the old ballads she sung around the house had a tremendous impact on his own writing. He remembered vividly "Old King Cole" which she voiced to him in his childhood. And another, Frederick Clay's setting to W.G. Wills's words, "I'll sing thee songs of Araby," was, to Weatherly, "surely the most beautiful love song ever written."

Throughout his autobiography, Weatherly refers to his mother's voice as a poignant and lasting reminder of the love they shared. Decades after her death, he included the Portishead newspaper's glowing obituary of her in his book, painting a keenly felt portrait of the woman who enchanted him with music. Throughout *Piano and Gown*, Weatherly wrote of instances where he imagined his mother's voice, singing the words he wrote in moments of inspiration, even into the twilight of his writing career. Indeed, many of his songs appear to have been written from the point of view of a loving mother to a beloved son.

Weatherly was the first to admit that his lyrics were romantic and sentimental and he had too much respect for the poets he admired to compare his work to theirs. He maintained a "humble hope" that he, too, would write words which accomplished composers would set to music and illustrious singers would make their own.

"I thought to myself," he wrote, "if my words shall be good enough for that there will be something in them."

In *Piano and Gown*, Weatherly recounted what inspired him as a lyricist. It's hard not to recall the scenery and emotion of "Danny Boy" when he observes:

> FRIENDS OFTEN ASK ME HOW I WRITE MY SONGS,
> WHERE DO I FIND MY SUBJECTS? ARE THEY HISTO-
> RIES OF ACTUAL FACTS? THOSE ARE QUESTIONS
> WHICH ARE DIFFICULT IF NOT IMPOSSIBLE TO
> ANSWER EXCEPT VAGUELY. SOMETHING SEEN,
> SOMETHING READ OF, SOMETHING TOLD; SOME
> TRAGEDY, SOME COMEDY OF LIFE OF WHICH ONE
> HAS HEARD OR IN WHICH ONE HAS TAKEN A PART;
> KNOWLEDGE OF PEOPLE'S WAYS AND PECULIARITIES;
> LOVE OF BEAUTIFUL THINGS, THE SEA, THE FORESTS,
> THE ROLLING HILLS, THE WAKING VOICES OF THE
> DAWN, THE SOLEMN HUSH OF NIGHT, ALL THESE
> THINGS AND THE POWER TO APPRECIATE THEM GO
> TO THE MAKING OF SONGS.

Weatherly had an enormous amount of respect for songs that people love. They may not have been labeled *artistic* or *shop ballads* by music critics, but he recognized "the heart of the people is still simple and healthy and sound," and he admits he wished he had been the author of many more popular songs.

By 1887, Weatherly had tired of the drudgery of coaching at Oxford. When he received his call to the Bar at the Inner Temple, he took chambers in London with Henry Dickens, son of the eminent novelist. The two never discussed literature or music, and funneled all their energies into the practice of law. However, Weatherly provedto be a prolific lyricist in his spare time, writing on trains to some distant court, or in the court itself, waiting for a trial to open. Can you imagine a song as heartbreaking and emotional as "Danny Boy" being put to paper on a jostling train by a man in a suit and briefcase, on his way to attend to the morning's motions and proceedings? I can't, frankly. I would like to think that an elegant and plaintive Weatherly managed to locate some shade beneath a tree one sunny English day, where he poured himself a cup of tea, surveyed the rolling hills and realized a moment of inspiration. I'd like to believe that. More likely, though, he jotted out some tentative lines while waiting for a judge to pass sentence on some poor sod on trial for some ordinary crime. If so, it certainly offers a new and slightly sadistic meaning to the first verse, if one could envision "pipes" as a slang term for prison bars!

We can debate whether "Danny Boy" is a farewell from a lover, father or mother into eternity. However, it is relevant to note that Weatherly often wrote songs from the point of view of the opposite sex. "The Glory of the Sea" is a lover's lament of her man lost at sea, and it echoes some of the same themes in "Danny Boy":

> *O get you home, brave sailor!*
> *Good night, and let me be!*
> *Thank God I gave my dearest*
> *To the Glory of the sea!*

> *And there he's safely sleeping*
> *In God Almighty's keeping,*
> *Till the sound of the last Trumpet*
> *Shall give him back to me!*

It is only the line,

> *And did you see the gray ship*
> *That took my man from me?*

that alludes to a woman longing for her man, but as with many of Weatherly's lyrics, this ambiguity can be explained by the habit of lyricists at the time to write songs for either male or female singers, thus potentially doubling the buying public for sheet music sales.

Weatherly joined the Local Bar in Bristol in 1893 and though he enjoyed success in his practice, he maintained his enthusiasm for writing lyrics. The beginning of World War I inspired Weatherly to plumb the kind of passion and tragedy that only wartime can convey. In the same romantic and heroic vein as "Danny Boy," he wrote "The Deathless Army":

> *Marching for the dear Old Country,*
> *Leading us for evermore,*
> *For the souls of the heroes die not,*
> *In the land that they adore!*

The other song which gained Fred a lot of notice and quite a bit of money was "Roses of Picardy." It turned out to be a huge hit with the troops and their left-behind loves during World War I. Written in 1916, it proved, beyond a shadow of a doubt, that our man liked roses:

> *She is watching by the poplars,*
> *Colinette with the sea-blue eyes,*
> *She is watching and longing and waiting,*

*Where the long white roadway lies.*
*And a song stirs in the silence,*
*As the wind in the boughs above,*
*She listens and starts and trembles,*
*'Tis the first little song of love:*
*Roses are shining in Picardy,*
*In the hush of the silver dew,*
*Roses are flow'ring in Picardy,*
*But there's never a rose like you!*
*And the roses will die with the summertime,*
*And our roads may be far apart,*
*But there's one rose that dies Not in Picardy!*
*'Tis the rose that I keep in my heart!*

*And the years fly on forever,*
*Till the shadows veil their skies,*
*But he loves to hold her little hands,*
*And Look in her sea-blue eyes.*
*And she sees the road by the poplars,*
*Where they met in the bygone years,*
*For the first little song of the roses*
*Is the last little song she hears:*

*Roses are shining in Picardy,*
*In the Hush of the silver dew,*
*Roses are flow'ring in Picardy,*
*But there's never a rose like you!*

*And the roses will die with the summertime,*
*And our roads may be far apart,*
*But there's one rose that dies Not in Picardy!*
*'Tis the rose that I keep In my heart!*

As we now know, Weatherly did not intend for the lyrics of "Danny Boy" to accompany the Londonderry air originally. He had another composition in mind when he wrote it in 1910, but the song never got attention, and so he filed it away for a couple of years. In 1912, however, his sister-in-law loved the melody, which she probably discovered in either Australian Percy Grainger's arrangement of the Londonderry air, or George Petrie's *Ancient Music of Ireland*. She sent it to Weatherly in England, feeling only he could do the beautiful tune justice. Although charmed by the air, Fred did not see the need to write something specific for it. Instead, he realized that he had written a song several years before which fit the melody perfectly, with only the need for a few minor alterations, and just like that, "Danny Boy" was reborn.

It was not likely that Weatherly's in-law was aware of the fact that many poets and writers, including Thomas Moore, Alfred Perceval Graves, Edward Lawson, and some ninety-plus others, had transcribed words to this melody. All other versions quickly evaporated and "Danny Boy" evolved into the accepted lyrics to the air. Graves, author of "Trottin' to the Fair" and a friend of Weatherly, apparently hit the overhanging eaves in rage when he learned that his old pal was co-opting this public domain tune. Alfred didn't think it sporting of Fred, and it led to a sundering of the friendship. It seems as if Weatherly always had his finger on the sensitive pulse of his fellow humans, which made him an effective barrister as well as a songwriter. When the music publisher Boosey of Boosey and Hawkes in London accepted "Danny Boy" for publication, it caught the public's immediate attention. Europe maintained its usual ferment, with war clouds darkening the sky, raising the possibility of young men marching off to war. "Danny Boy," with his pipes and his call to duty and departure, developed into a hymn hummed with epic sadness across the British Isles. They crooned other songs, too, like "It's a Long Way to Tiperrary," "There Is an Isle," "There's a Long Long Trail a Winding," "Keep the Home Fires Burning," "Roses of Picardy," and "Lily Marlene." But "Danny Boy" whipped the masses into a sentimental clutch, and as Fred was too elderly to go to war, he stayed home and collected his royalties on the sheet music and performances.

Weatherly did not have much to say about the writing of or inspiration behind "Danny Boy," or the song's profound effect on the public. In 1926, when he wrote his autobiography, the song, although popular, had not yet reached the level of immortality that it ultimately achieved. But he did make very telling statements about his work at various points in his life. On one occasion in the twilight of his years, Weatherly was asked to give "The Immortal Memory," a traditional speech at a dinner with The Burns Society, which usually included the most celebrated musicians and songwriters in Europe at the time. Weatherly had strong feelings about the impact of songs, and in his address to The Burns Society, he reveals the passion that must have stirred him when creating "Danny Boy." In *Piano and Gown*, he recalls the speech:

SONG AND STORY ARE INDEED CLOSELY CONNECTED. A SONG, AS IT SEEMS TO ME, IS A SHORT POEM WHICH EITHER TELLS A SIMPLE STORY OR EXPRESSES A SIMPLE IDEA. AND IT IS DIFFICULT TO FIND A SONG WHICH IS NOT AT THE SAME TIME A STORY. A SONG EITHER SUGGESTS MUSIC OR IS SUGGESTED BY MUSIC, AND IT IS PERFECTLY CERTAIN THAT IT IS UPON THE WINGS OF MUSIC THAT SONGS BEST REACH THE

HEART. ONE OF THE FEATURES OF THE SONGS OF
BURNS, SELDOM NOTICED BY HIS MOST ARDENT
WORSHIPPERS, IS THAT THE MAJORITY OF THEM WERE
WRITTEN TO FIT THE OLD NATIONAL MELODIES OF
SCOTLAND, PROVING THAT HE WAS NOT ONLY A POET
BUT A MUSICIAN. I LOVED THE SONGS OF BURNS
WHEN FIRST MY MOTHER SANG THEM; AND BECAUSE
IT WAS SHE WHO SANG THEM, MY EARLIEST AND
PERHAPS MY ONLY AMBITION WAS THAT SOMEDAY I,
TOO, MIGHT WRITE SONGS. OXFORD, TO MY SURPRISE
AND DISAPPOINTMENT, TOLD ME THAT THE SONGS OF
BURNS WERE NOT CLASSIC, AND WERE NOT EVEN
WORTHY TO BE CALLED LITERATURE; AND IT WAS
RESERVED FOR THIS GREAT CITY OF COMMERCE
(BRISTOL) TO SHOW ME THE MEANING OF THE CULT
OF BURNS. IT WAS A HAPPY HOUR THAT BROUGHT ME
BACK TO SETTLE IN MY COUNTRY OF THE WEST, TO
WALK ONCE MORE OVER THE GREEN HILLS OF
SOMERSET, TO DREAM AGAIN OF ARTHUR AND OF
AVALON, TO SEE AGAIN IN THE FANCY THE EARLIEST
CHRISTIAN CHURCH PLANTED BY JOSEPH. WHY IS IT
THAT SONGS APPEAL? IS THERE NOT A STORY IN
EACH? A MELODY WHICH REMAINS DEEP DOWN IN
OUR HEARTS? WE MAY LISTEN TO THE NOBLEST

SERMONS. WE MAY STUDY THE DEEPEST PHILOSOPHY.
WE MAY BE ELEVATED BY THE LOFTIEST SPEECHES.
WE MAY READ THE BRIGHTEST PAGES OF HISTORY.
AND YET NONE APPEAL TO US WITH QUITE THE SAME
APPEAL AS SONG AND STORY. IS IT NOT PERHAPS THAT
ALL THE REST APPEAL TO THE INTELLECT AND NEED
MENTAL POWERS WHICH ONLY THE FEW POSSESS?
BUT SONG AND STORY APPEAL TO THE HEART. FROM
THE HEART THEY COME AND TO THE HEART THEY GO.
THEY EXPRESS THE JOYS AND SORROWS OF THE POET
HIMSELF; AND JUST BECAUSE HE IS A POET THEY
EXPRESS THE JOYS AND SORROWS OF THE WORLD.
THINK TO-NIGHT OF THE MILLIONS WHO ARE
SINGING SONGS, NOT MERELY ON THIS FESTIVAL
NIGHT OF THE GREATEST SONG WRITER OF THE
WORLD. TO-NIGHT AND EVERY NIGHT, WHEN THE
SONGS OF THE BIRDS ARE SILENT AND THE STEPS OF
THE PASSERS ARE HUSHED IN THE STREET; IN ALL
PLACES, HIGH AND LOWLY, IN CIRCUMSTANCES COM-
MONPLACE AND IN THE MOST TRAGIC MOMENTS,
SONGS ARE BEING SUNG. THOSE WHO WENT FROM
THAT UPPER CHAMBER TO THE GREATEST TRAGEDY
OF THE WORLD SANG A HYMN BEFORE THEY WENT;
PAUL AND SILAS SANG HYMNS IN PRISON; WHEN THE

GREAT SHIP SETTLES DOWN TO HER DOOM, WHEN
THE LAST MOMENT IN THE BELEAGUERED FORT HAS
COME, WHEN THE ENTOMBED MINER KNOWS THERE
IS NO ESCAPE; IT IS NOT ARGUMENT, IT IS NOT PHI-
LOSOPHY, IT IS NOT DOGMAS THAT STRENGTHEN
AND CONSOLE THEM; IT IS THE SONGS AND PSALMS
AND HYMNS THEY LEARNT FROM THE DEAREST LIPS
OF ALL. IT IS THESE THAT COME BACK TO THEM IN
THEIR LAST MOMENTS.

Frederick Weatherly died in 1929, leaving behind a collection of over 1,500 published verses, translated operas,
and children's books. But his "humble hope" of someday
writing words for songs that "great singers would
sing"was more than realized in "Danny Boy."

# The
## pipes
### are
### calling

# The Questions

"*D*anny Boy" isn't as well worn as that bit of dogged verse known as "Happy Birthday." Conversely, the latter hardly has a reputation for reducing a room to tears, so I'll leave it to scholars to determine which song has more social significance. At any given time of the day, somewhere in the world, some homesick boy is humming this haunting tune or some girl is singing it, because her love departed for a life in the armed services. Mothers croon it too, regretting that they did not name the absent lad Danny when he was born.

In verse poetry, in story, or in song, it's no easy task to find sagas of mothers, daughters, and sisters heading for the battlefield, the ocean deep, the towering mountain, or the blistering hot desert. But the annals are replete with departures of the boys or male members of the family. Despite the evocation of sadness, of anguished farewells, indeed of the finality of death itself, why does the song gain new, adoring, mournful acolytes each year? With so many songs carrying the same theme, why has this one remained in the collective psyche of the world as the preeminent song of a tearful farewell?

What does "Irish" conjure up in the mind of any man or any woman with a hint of romance or a trace of poetry in the soul? Few will dispute the lure and charm and wonder of all things connected with that green island across the sea. It seems only right that the journey into the mystery that is "Danny Boy" commence there. Despite centuries of warfare, revolution, insurgency, and rebellion against the Sassanach invader, the land is unspoiled and the forty shades of green vie and yet merge together in a restful, soothing palate.

Some are convinced the Irish are not serious about anything other than saying goodbye. Death is accepted, so is battle, the loss of spouse, even the dying of children. Tragedy seems indigenous to the land. It was always a puzzle to the English that in the midst of grief, in the midst of carnage, the Irish man could leap to his feet and give vent to a full-throated song or an intricate story, even ones with comic overtones. G.K. Chesterton was compelled to put pen to paper and write a small poem that is now cliché:

*The great Gaels of Ireland*
*Are men that God made mad*
*For all their wars are merry*
*And all their songs are sad.*

Perhaps old G.K. was influenced by the fact that the ancient Celts fought all their wars in their pelts, as they say in rural areas. (To those not in the know, that means naked.) To face a fully-clad warrior or an armored knight might be intimidating enough, but to face a man wearing only his skin is apt to stir speculation that the opposing force is composed of lunatics who fear nothing.

Of course, there is nothing merry about a war, and of course not all Irish songs are sad. Non-Irish lyricists, such as the American, Chauncey Olcott, author of "When Irish Eyes are Smiling" and "My Wild Irish Rose" tend toward the over-romantic and sad, whereas native Irish can be satirical and rely on irony, qualities largely absent in the English psyche. Thus, the most sentimental of self-styled Irish songs were concocted by songwriters like Edgar "Yip" Harburg, who were visitors to the Emerald Isle and for a brief moment, amble into the Celtic twilight. Melodies will ring in their heads and they will write words intended to requite this new and insistent love. No words will suffice, however, and the writer is left with a void in the heart. Almost all the songs of longing, of leaving, and of hoping to return are soft and melodic, even a faux Irish song like Harburg's, "How are Things in Glocca Morra?" Other popular songs of that genre include "I'll Take You Home Again Kathleen," "Galway Bay," "Hills of Donegal," "Home to Mayo," and the subject of this small tome. Even songs of protest and of war are rounded with melody, which make them singable, despite their minor keys. Furthermore, the Irish speak melodically, so melodically that it is often difficult to know when one has been insulted. There are subversive songs, such as "Moses Ritooral Ritoorilay" and "Mother England Loves Us Still" which were dismissed by the British as childish doggerel, not knowing that their imperialistic rule was mocked by Irish laughter.

Oddly enough, the Irish are susceptible to the weepy warblings of such foreigner drivel as "McNamara's Band," "Christmas in Killarney," and again, that geographically-challenged "Glocca Morra" stream that ventures east, north, and south at the same time, spanning hundreds of miles because the town names happen to rhyme. It would be hard to pick the winner of the competition for allegedly Irish claptrap, but George M. Cohan certainly counts among the medalists. He specialized in the stereotype of the nationalistic, swaggering Irish buffoon, and his trite song, "Harrigan," is not likely to be included in any time capsules documenting stellar Irish contributions to civilization. There is no hint of the poet here, nor of the intelligent and artistic men and women who painted, sculpted, and published books; no sign of the quiet men who took over the political system, the ones who never drank whiskey and never gave a speech.

The stage Irishman was Cohan's forte, and perhaps he served a purpose, as he did his strutting and singing while the peaceful men stealthily undermined the WASP structures. The opposite sex was relegated to cheeky, sharp-tongued, but virginal women, shackled by male lust and in perpetual need of counsel from Fathers Murphy, Flanagan, O'Brien, or any other celibate round-collar in the vicinity.

I don't know how many Irish songs concern mother, but they must number in the hundreds. My brother Frank claims that we were trapped in a territory of maternities, Mother Ireland, Mother Church, as well as the songs, "That Old Irish Mother of Mine" and "Mother Machree." Machree comes from the Gaelic *mo croide* (of the heart).

Foreign sentimentalists such as Cohan were also likely to have the little old Irish mother lingering at the cottage door, with its thatched roof, white-washed walls and roses twined on trellises around the door, tearfully waving to the parting son. A young girl would never get the same send-off as the boy. Very few of the songs describe a female departure, though they left Ireland to be housemaids and farm girls in distant America, suffering the same hardships and deprivations as the boys. But where are the songs? There are the Kathleen songs (Caitlin being the correct name in Irish), as well as the innumerable Rose and Rosalee songs. Yet many of these were merely pseudonyms for Ireland, as it was seditious under British law to sing of fighting for or loving that country.

Before The Great Hunger, sometimes incorrectly called The Famine, in the 1840s, the Irish subsisted on the potato, as it keeps for quite a long time in the winter months. And there were paeans to that humble tuber too, i.e. "The Garden Where the Praties Grow" and the very somber "Famine Song":

> *We are down into the dust*
> *Over here, over here*

*We are down into the dust*
*Over here, over here*
*We are down into the dust*
*But the Lord in Whom we trust*
*Will repay us crumb for crust*
*Over here, over here.*

Songs and poems about the perfidious landlords stockpiling wheat, barley, oats, vegetables, and livestock, and exporting them to England whilst hundreds of thousands of Irish men, women, and children died of starvation and exposure after failing to pay rent, were rare. But The Great Starvation did not stop young men from planting the seeds of rebellion and revolution with one hand, while accepting the queen's shilling to quell uprisings elsewhere in the British Empire with the other. The sun never set on the British Empire, so the saying goes, because God could not trust the English in the dark.

What was there to sing about, then? The usual rage at the oppressor, self-imposed exile, and as always, fathers and mothers bidding goodbye to children, holding what were known as American wakes. Though the person was not dead, just emigrating, it was unlikely he would ever see the homeland again. So, as usual, the Irish sang, played fiddles and melodeons, and the music drowned out the imminent truth of a necessary departure. As the morning drew nigh, the music slowed to a mournful dirge and the singing slipped from melody to the old practice of keening—a high wail. Then, other women joined in to extol the virtues and attributes of the dead or departing person. In the American wake, the reveler saw the traveler to the crossroads where the conveyance to the ship was awaiting, whilst the parents and siblings stayed in the home. If the emigrant was a boy and had a girlfriend she would often tuck one of her pubic hairs somewhere in his clothing, in the belief that this intimate object would preserve his chastity and faithfulness. It is not known how many songs of departure, emigration, and death the Irish gave vent to, but the chances of a young woman ever seeing her love again were remote, even if she planted a garden of her hairs in the lad's trousers or keened all the lamentations, sang all the songs, or plucked out every hair of her body, north or south, east or west, or any other point of the compass in the universe and beyond, as the Mayo man said when pressed to expand a thought.

Naturally, there are competing claimants to the origins of this old tune, melody, or air commonly known as the "Londonderry air." The prurient and prudish

Victorians were quite shy about calling it the "Londonderry air" because of the closeness in pronunciation to the French word "derriere." The preservation of propriety was of utmost importance; to the Victorians we owe the ordering of "white" and "dark" portions of the furtive fowl, as they demurred from saying "breast" or "thigh." Modesty and chastity, not to mention celibacy, were also maintained on the bookshelves of these pure people; they never allowed books by males and females in close proximity. So, 'twas a wonder that anything was written, or indeed published, except for the purest of drivel or jingoistic poems of praise for the soldiers who kept the British colonies in thrall. Perhaps Danny was one of those oppressors who had taken the Queen's shilling or the King's shilling. The name of the air itself may lend some insight as to who is offering the heart-wrenching farewell. When parents have to speak sternly to offspring, they will generally use the child's full name, Thomas or William instead of Tommy or Billy, threatening "Come here at once!" or "If you don't do your homework . . ." etc. The same technique is used by judges when sentencing convicted criminals to death, i.e. "George Walker Bush, I hereby sentence you to be hanged by the neck until you are dead!" etc. But diminutives of names bespeak affection and toleration for the naughtiness of children, which brings us to "Danny Boy."

It would be unseemly to call the lad Daniel, just as it would be unseemly to tell the story of Danny in the Lion's Den. And who could ever think of calling the late Mr. Webster "Danny" or Mr. Dafoe, or indeed Daniel O'Connell, who was known as "The Liberator" because he secured Catholic Emancipation for Ireland? The nickname wouldn't do for these austere gentlemen. But for Danny it's fine, for it would be rather hard to sing "Oh Daniel Boy," not to mention pompous and reproving. And so, we are wont to ask, why and how did Weatherly, who lived in England all of his born years, come to write the lyrics to a haunting melody, which causes tears to course down the cheeks of strong men and sends delicate slips of lovelorn ladies into paroxysms of grief, even though nobody in the immediate family has had the temerity to die, fight a war, or even holiday in a foreign country?

The allure of the lyrics arises from our ignorance of who is addressing said Danny, the details of the circumstances, and where this colloquy takes place. Is the lad spoken to from afar? Why does Danny not hear the pipes that are calling from glen to glen? Is there a recruiting sergeant roaming the country, accompanied by bagpipes? 'Tis often said that the Irish gave the bagpipes to the Scots, who have yet to see the joke! So, let us list all the candidates who might be bidding farewell to our hero Danny:

1. mother
2. father
3. wife
4. girlfriend
5. sister
6. brother
7. son
8. daughter
9. gay lover
10. parish priest

There is no logical way to disprove every theory to date, which renders the true meaning behind the words elusive, mirage-like, and just beyond our grasp. But one can formulate educated guesses by examining the clues within the words themselves.

To begin with, I think that we can eliminate the parish priest, as they are a notoriously unsentimental lot. But beyond that, the image of Danny (an altar boy perhaps?) returning to the grave in the second verse ventures far beyond the overly-sentimental, and reaches into the absurd, if not disturbing. At its purest intent, it's still a bad scene from a campy movie, and Danny certainly deserves a better fate than that.

It's shocking enough that the lyrics to "Danny Boy" were written by an Englishman, but try to imagine the look on the Ancient Order of Hibernians' faces at the next St. Patrick's Day parade were they to learn that this beloved song was an openly gay lover's lament to his companion, Danny. Implausible for many reasons, the least of which being that a married, middle-aged English barrister such as Weatherly, had not the slightest trace of homosexual content in his impressive collective. That is, if we ignore the most extreme of the Jack-the-Ripper conspiracy theories! More realistically, Fred was not likely to risk being ostracized for taking such a progressive social stand in the beginning of the twentieth century when he penned the lyrics. But giving Fred the benefit of the doubt by putting him ahead of his time, what are the odds, as stated in the second verse, of a gay lover coming home to dying flowers? Quite slim, I'd suspect. Clearly, the clues are written between the lines.

The daughter singing to dear old Dad doesn't work on several levels. Not only is there the problem of her addressing him by his first name in the song, but the likelihood of him outliving her and returning to her grave gives the song a less romantic and more maudlin tone that works against the author's language elsewhere. More plausible, perhaps, is the sister singing to her brother. But siblings in the Emerald Isle would not likely address each other in such formal or poetic tones.

And so we arrive at another thus far, the girlfriend. Now, if Danny were heading off across the briny during The Great Hunger of the 1840s, bound for America, 'tis unlikely that he would ever return. 'Twas said a gray-headed Irishman was a rare species as death visited most of them within fifteen years of arrival on the golden shores of Amerikay. And on further examination, destination America is a dubious assumption, 'cos it's pipes that are doing the calling. I assume that they are not the mere traditional non-militaristic elbow pipes (Uileann pipes) because you can't march about with these protuberances strapped to body and elbow. Furthermore, Pan pipes were not common to the area. The land described is inhospitable and intolerable, all mountains and glens, so that if the reason for leaving was economic, our man Danny would have brought the missus along for the crossing, as was often the case with family emigration from Ireland. So, that casts the wife scenario in suspicion.

Now we are left with the Ma and the Da, which

may prove the most likely of choices. Grand Irish tenors such as John McCormack were so convincing in their performances of "Danny Boy" that audiences were convinced the song was that of a father to a son. Aside from the paternal address ("Danny Boy"), there's a clear indication that Danny may be considerably younger than the narrator. For instance, it's assumed that when Danny returns, the narrator will likely be dead. Furthermore, the line, "It's you, it's you must go and I must bide" is consistent with a father's lament that he himself could not answer the call to battle, and that his son instead must heed the call of the pipes. But then, "Danny Boy" is entreated to return when the summer is in the meadow or when the valley is buried under snow, because he or she who was left behind will not have stirred.

So while the father as narrator is credible, one must question the prodigious affection he shows toward his son. Despite the effectiveness of the song when sung by a male, it is still hard to imagine an Irish father grasping for such sentimental and romantic words as established in the second verse, bidding Danny to "bend and tell me that you love me, And I shall sleep in peace until you come to me!"

Again, entirely within the realm of possibility,

and a case made all the more powerful under the spell of the Irish tenors. But as we've already established, the influence of Frederick Weatherly's mother on his writing is formidable, and from the evidence, it appears Weatherly wrote the lyrics as if his mother were the narrator. He then attempted to neutralize the gender-specific language, crafting a song more suitable for both sexes.

Weatherly's lyrics also hint at the time, place, and setting of the song, as well as some background on the parties involved. In the second verse there are the lines, "Ye'll come and find the place where I am lying and kneel and say an Ave there for me." Note that the lines don't ask for a prayer, but an Ave, which is the clue to the religion of the folks in this miniature saga of goodbye, death, and return. An "Ave" usually precedes "Maria" (as written by Gounod) and the woman Maria is the mother of Jesus, to whom any average Church of Rome adherents have more than a passing devotion. The conclusion: all of the participants in this epic, above and below ground, are of the Catholic faith.

Most ghost stories concern spirits haunting a particular spot where a violent act occurred, such as murder, battle, or suicide. Shakespeare's plays are replete with such ghosts, as in *Hamlet* and *Macbeth*. Sometimes in a story of unrequited love, a grief-stricken maiden will weep for the return of a lover, even though he may be dead. Buried, the deceased is stretched out in a posture of waiting in hopes of a warmer, sweeter grave, if such a thing is possible with decay and decomposition. Some revisionists, perhaps disturbed by Weatherly's morbidity, have tried to change the original words from "And all my grave shall warmer, sweeter be" to "And all my dreams will warm and sweeter be." Indeed, there are many recordings with the softer, more romantic phrasing of "Danny Boy." However, we will entertain facts and flights of fancy, but no changes in the original text.

So despite all the analysis and assumptions, the song has all the remnants of a mystery, although perfectly pieced together so as to seize the hearts of so many, and yet so cryptically phrased as to preserve it as a secret.

*The valley's hushed and white with snow*

# The Land of
Derry

What is it about Derry or Londonderry to put an air to? The town maintains historic political implications, even the name itself. (Protestant loyalists call it Londonderry, Catholic nationalists call it Derry.) Our Londonderry or Derry is a city in the province of Ulster, located in the northernmost part of Ireland. The whole country is divided into four provinces, the aforementioned Ulster to the north, Leinster in the east, Connaught to the west, and Munster to the south. These provinces, in turn, are divided into counties, thirty-two in all, of which six are part of Ulster and under British rule. Long ago, the rebellious Northern Irish resisted British rule, provoking fears of a revolution. After an abortive and prolonged war on the invaders, the O'Neills and the O'Donnells were defeated and went off into exile in Italy and Spain. Their lands were confiscated and given to Scots Presbyterians who, it was assumed, were better farmers than the natives. The Irish retreated to the hills and mountains and in furious raging raids, they attempted to kill off the usurpers, much the same as the Indians did in America. 'Twas thus they gained a reputation for savagery and later, terrorism.

That area of Ireland produced not only warriors, but bards and poets. It also provided the setting for one of the greatest Irish epics known as the Cattle Raid of Cooley and the death of the mythical hero Cuchulainn. An ancient poem, "Summer is Gone," sometimes attributed to Finn, and sometimes listed as Anonymous in the ninth century, laments the passing of the summer:

*I have tidings for you: the stag bells; winter pours;*
*summer has gone;*
*Wind is high and cold; the sun low; its course is short*
*the sea runs strongly;*
*Bracken is very red; its shape has been hidden; the call*
*Of the barnacle-goose has become usual;*
*Cold has seized the wings of birds; season of ice: these are my tidings.*

Another poem from the same period also associates aging and death with the change of seasons:

[1st verse]

*Winter is cold; the wind has risen: the fierce stark-wild*

*Stag arises; not warm tonight is the unbroken mountain,*
*Even though the swift stag be belling.*

[5th verse]
*Today I am old and aged: few men do I recognize;*
*I used to brandish a pointed spear hardily on a morning of truly*
*cold ice.*

We are left to look not only on the history and birthplace of this melody, but on the inhabitants as well. Despite the second verse's finality, there are numerous songwriters, poets, and patriots who passionately desire to clarify this song by injecting nationalism and militarism with additional verses of "Danny Boy." I'm indebted to Michael Robinson and his Standing Stones Web site for the following verses, which he says claim no paternity:

*Oh Danny Boy, go bravely fight*
*for freedom*
*My beloved child I give to Mother*
*Ireland*
*For it was she who gave him*
*unto me*
*A hundred sons though they be*
*taken from me*

*And if for Erin's cause they too must*
*Die*
*God's hands will surely guide them*
*Unto glory*
*As upon the holy battlefield*
*They lie.*

At times this will cause eyes to roll skyward and evoke unprintable expletives. A cursory survey of women who are mothers was inconclusive, but hilarious, nonetheless. My poll was not scientific by any means, but the sentiments were clear. To the question "Would you give your son to die for Ireland, or indeed America?" the replies were mixed: "Have you seen a doctor lately?" "I couldn't give him to anyone. He's too rowdy," "No, he always comes home for dinner," and so on.

Furthermore, if the mothers ever did manage to bring a hundred sons into the world, they wouldn't mind ninety-seven or so joining the army, provided they avoided an actual war. Unanimously, the mothers were unable to reconcile the words "holy" and "battlefield" and believed it unlikely that God would approve of death in the name of war.

Another verse harkens back to simpler times when gunpowder was unavailable to the revolting peasantry:

*But should I live and should you*
*Die for Ireland*
*Let not your dying thoughts be*
*All of me*
*But breathe a prayer to God for*
*Our dear Sireland*
*That He will hear and He will set her*
*Free*
*And I will take your place and pike*
*My dearest*
*And strike a blow, though weak*
*That blow may be*
*To help the cause to which your heart was nearest*
*and you will rest in Peace until I come for thee*

Once more, a warlike parent dispatches a son to spill blood for Ireland. And in the best traditions of martyred motherhood, she enjoins him not to think of her as the blood bubbles around his lips in his last moment of life. Rather, Danny should be praying "for our dear Sireland." Note the gender change from Mother Ireland to Sireland. Bad poets will sacrifice anything for a rhyme.

Further along in the verse, the bloodlust has overtaken the poor woman as she is ready to whack the nearest Englishman with a pike. This, despite the fact that the pike is more a spear-like weapon, practical for impaling or penetrating an enemy, but somewhat inept in the whacking department.

As Michael Robinson said, the image of Danny's gray-haired mother in her black-tasseled shawl, tottering off to war with a big pike to turn the red coats into shishkabobs, is fairly ludicrous. Historically, the women did do their part in defending the country, particularly at the Siege of Limerick in 1651, where they threw stones at the Cromwell army. Nearly forty years later in 1689, the Siege of Derry began, and once more the Irish were forced to take sides in the complicated politics and wars of continental Europe. James II, a Catholic, had antagonized the Protestant power elite in Britain by ceding Ireland to his brother-in-law, Tyrconnell, who restored Catholics to full participation. Outraged, the Protestants implored William of Orange to oust Jimmy II and restore Protestant values, and so the war commenced. And where did this war, The Willimaite War as it came to be known, begin? Why, in the land of Danny Boy, of course.

This ancient city of Derry was the site of a monastery founded by the great Irish scholar St. Colmcille around the fifth century. The word *Derry* derives from theGaelic word *doire*, which means "oak tree." The whole of the island of Ireland was covered by oak forests and when a tree grew close to a well, it became a holy place where ribbons and adornments and later on, medals were hung in supplication to the spirits who resided there. In the numerous uprisings and revolutions that occurred after the English pope, Adrian IV, granted dominion over Ireland to Henry II, oak forests provided ideal hiding places for the rebellious Irish engaged in guerilla warfare. But the Brits had a judicious response to the pesky problem of these mighty oaks. They knocked 'em down, an effective tactic of deforestation and defoliation which preceeded the United States's own chemical version, centuries later, in Vietnam. Besides flushing out the mad Irish from their lairs, the English used the oak to build the grand ships of the British navy and to line the interiors of their majestic cathedrals, for the glory of God and the rule of Brittania. Because of the desecration and destruction of the sacred oak tree, Doire has immeasurable significance for the Irish.

Derry City has a history as one of the most attacked and besieged cities. Though the area was occupied for several thousands of years, it was not until the summer of 1600 that the foundation stones for the modern city were laid by a force commanded by Sir Henry Docwra. The following is an excerpt from *The History of Ulster* by Jonathan Bardon from the Narration of Sir Henry Docwra:

ON THE 22ND OF MAY WEE PUT THE ARMY IN ORDER TO MARCHE, & LEAVING CAPTAIN LANCELLOTT ATFORD AT CULMORE WITH 600 MEN, TO MAKE UP THE WORKES, WEE WENT TO THE DERRY 4 MYLES OF UPON THE RIVER SIDE, A PLACE IN MAN NER OF AN ILAND COMPREHENDING WITHIN IT 40 ACRES OF GROUND, WHEREIN WERE THE RUINES OF AN OLD ABBAY, OF A BISHOPP'S HOUSES, OF TWO CHURCHES, & AT OF THE ENDS OF IT AN OLD CASTLE, THE RIVER CALLED LOUGHFOYLE ENCOMPASSING IT ALL ON ONE SIDE, & A BOGG MOST COMMONLIE WETT, & NOT EASILIE PASSABLE EXCEPT IN TWO OR THREE PLACES DIVIDING IT FROM THE MAINE LAND.

THIS PEECE OF GROUND WE POSSEST OUR SELVES OF WITHOUT RESISTAUNCE, & JUDGING IT A FITT PLACE TO MAKE OUR MAINE PLANTATION IN, BEING SOME WHAT HIE, & THEREFORE DRY, & HELATHIE TO DWELL UPON, ATT THAT END WHERE THE OLD CASTLE

STOOD, BEING CLOSER TO THE WATER SIDE, I
PRESENTLIE RESOLVED TO RAISE A FFORTE TO KEEP
OUR STOORE OF MUNITION & VICTUELLS IN, & IN
THE OTHER A LITTLE ABOVE WHERE THE WALLS OF
AN OLD CATHEDRAL CHURCH WERE YET STANDING
TO EVERT ANOTHER FOR OUR FUTURE SAFETIE &
RETREATE UNTO UPON ALL OCCASSIONS.

James II, whose daughter Mary was married to his enemy,
William of Orange, ordered the Protestant soldiers out of
Derry, replacing them with a Catholic regiment. The
town's leading citizens fervently discussed whether to
comply with this edict. A fearful Bishop Hopkins advised
that surrender would be the best course, a notion backed
by a trembling bunch of city fathers. However, an intrep-
id lot of apprentice boys, thirteen in all, stole the keys of
the gates from the guards and raised the main drawbridge.
They locked the gates with yells of no surrender on their
lips and commenced a way of life, that in a sense, has last-
ed to this very day. Every year, on the nearest Saturday to
August 12th, thousands of men of all ages, calling themselves Apprentice Boys, commemorate the original thirteen boys with flags flying, drums beating, bellowing "No
surrender!" They march in the low-lying vicinity of the

Catholic area, and from the walls they throw pennies at the papists, a gesture of supreme contempt aimed at the cowering minority. Then it's off to the pubs to sing the battle songs and hymns of old and propose mad toasts, the more traditional one:

*Here's to the glorious immortal and pious memory*
*of King William,*
*who saved us from knaves and knavery, slaves and slavery,*
*rogues and roguery, brass money and wooden shoes!*
*If any man will not rise to this toast,*
*may he be slammed, crammed, and jammed*
*into the great gun of Athlone*
*and may that gun be fired into the pope's belly*
*and may the pope be fired into the devil's belly*
*and the devil fired into the deepest, darkest pits of hell,*
*and may the gates of hell be slammed shut and locked*
*and the key be kept for all eternity*
*in the pocket of an Orangeman*
*and here's a fart for the Bishop of Cork.*

Although knowing it would be difficult to top a fart for the Bishop of Cork, the Catholics managed a response of their own:

*Do not speak of your*
*Protestant minister*
*Or your church without morals or faith*
*For the foundation stones*
*Of your temple*
*Are the balls of Henry*
*the Eighth*

In the three hundred plus years since the Siege of Derry, emotions blaze up as if it were yesterday.

The people of Derry suffered dreadful privations. The constant bombardment brought buildings down on top of the women and children sheltering there. Here was the last fortified city in Europe enduring the last great siege of the British Empire. Involved in the struggle was the Pope James II, Leopold I of Austria, Maxmillian of Bavaria, Louis XIV of France, and any other available monarch with an unemployed army. Did the Irish Protestants or Catholics know that they were miserable, disposable pawns in an international quarrel among foreign kings? Not bloody likely. Just mention God, country, and principle, and it's no bother exciting people about preserving what never was.

This Siege of Derry dragged on for four months; the number of people who died from warfare and starvation cannot be counted, only estimated. According to Jonathan Borden in his "History of Ulster," there were seven thousand soldiers defending the city and as many as thirty thousand civilians clambering for safety. The soldiers were commanded by a Major Henry Baker and a Church of Ireland rector named George Walker, which causes one to wonder if he has a descendant who is a sitting president of the U.S.A.

While the rain of bombshells and cannonballs failed to damage the walls, it ravaged buildings and snuffed out many lives. The brave women defenders injected themselves into the fray by heaving stones at attackers who attempted to scale the walls. George Walker did his best to preserve stability within the walls, posting a price list of meats in a place where the starving defenders devoured everything except each other:

Horse flesh: one shilling eight pence per pound.

Quarter of a dog: five shilling six pence.

(Fattened by eating the bodies of dead Irish)

Dog's head: two shillings six pence.

A cat: four shillings six pence.

A rat: one shilling.

A mouse: six pence.

A fish: Priceless.

Considering that a shilling amounted to a week's wages, that was an awful lot of money for a bit of flesh. Fever wiped out most of the children. It was estimated that the total mortality of the Siege of Derry numbered fifteen thousand people. After 105 days, the siege was lifted when the defenders were relieved by ships sailing up the river Foyle, and Derry, in the words of Captain Ashe, thanked "the lord who has preserved this city from the enemy. I hope he will always keep it to the Protestants." God did for many years "keep it to the Protestants" with the help of odd laws and political gerrymandering, but today it is governed by a mostly nationalistic city council, and the name Derry has superseded the old name of Londonderry. In spite of that power shift, another enormous tragedy lay grinning in the dark, centuries later, awaiting the call to grisly duty.

On August 9th, 1971, the British government arrested 350 men suspected of IRA activities and on that day, the policy of internment without trial had begun. In a move designed to crush the IRA, anybody could be flung into the pokey on the suspicion of a senior police official. Mostly young Catholic men felt the brunt of this nefarious policy, and just six months after the policy was implemented, nearly 1,000 men had been jailed.

So it was that on Sunday, 30th January 1972, the NICRA (North Ireland Civil Rights Association) called for a massive demonstration in Derry, protesting the jail without trial policy. The government refused to issue a permit and banned the protest. The NICRA responded defiantly, stating that the protest would go forward, like it or not, and the government responded by putting men of the Parachute Regiment on duty to quell the prospective marchers. As a civil rights march, it emulated the strategies and tactics of Reverend Martin Luther King Jr., used so effectively in the United States. The organizers were eager to protest in peace, even singing "We Shall Overcome." The police were, for the most part, keeping things calm, but the paratroopers were a bit trigger-happy. Twenty thousand people assembled on that day and marched and sang with little resistance, except for a few rough encounters. But as the march was reaching its conclusion at around 4 p.m., the soldiers began shooting real bullets into the crowd, injuring a goodly group and killing thirteen males, seven of whom were under the age of eighteen. Lord Widgery, who presided over the official inquiry, noted that the shooting apparently bordered on the reckless, the usual bit of droll English understatement. Major Hubert O'Neill, the Derry coroner, concluded that the young men were shot in the back and that the army had slaughtered innocent people. In his statement of August 21, 1973, he wrote, "I would say without hesitation that it was sheer, unadulterated murder."

Once more, the flowers of Derry were dying. As Irish youths collapsed the pipes were calling for the Danny Boys who perished on Bloody Sunday. Nearly thirty years have passed since that fateful day in Irish history, and not a single person has been tried for the shooting of these innocent men in Derry.

Tell me that you love me

# The Pop History
## of "Danny Boy"

*T*o merely review the list of those who sang "Danny Boy," the fiddlers who played it, the groups who performed it, or orchestras that trumpeted it, boggles the mind. Each year, it seems, another superb rendition joins a list that already includes the likes of Black 47, Harry Belafonte, Count Basie, Ruben Blades, Johnny Cash, Rosemary Clooney, Judy Collins, and Morton Downey Sr., to name but a few.

"Danny Boy" is unique in that people are willing to overlook a bad rendition if the singer is earnest and the moment is true. Take, for instance, the boxer, Jack Doyle, nicknamed "The Gorgeous Gael," who gained the love and respect of the Irish in the 1930s when he fought for the British heavyweight title against Jack Peterson. Although Doyle was disqualified in the second round for committing a low blow, the flagrant foul failed to quell his popularity, even after his next fight when he was knocked out in the first round by Buddy Baer. Before long, Doyle acquired a new, less flattering nickname,"Canvas Back Jack," because he spent the majority of his time in the ring in the horizontal position.

What endeared fight fans and the Irish in general was Doyle's struggle to gain consciousness, when he would lumber to his feet and offer a bleary-eyed rendition of "Danny Boy" for his loyal fight fans. The sweet science had not yet taken its toll on Doyle's faculties. He wisely retired from boxing and married Movita, the Mexican starlet, and the two moved to England and embarked on a career as a singing act. A few years after their marriage, Doyle and Movita returned to Ireland, marrying again at St. Andrew's Catholic Church in Dublin in a firestorm of publicity that further elevated Doyle's status. However, in 1945, Movita left Doyle for Marlon Brando, and "The Gorgeous Gael" returned to London for a short-lived career as a wrestler before dying in poverty in 1978.

In the 1980s there was another Irish boxer, Barry McGuigan, ("The Clones Cyclone") who ignited a sensation in Ireland when he fought for the featherweight championship in June of 1985. His opponent was Panamanian Eusebio Pedroza, who held the World Boxing Association's featherweight title for years, successfully defending it 19 straight times. The 23-year-old

McGuigan, despite fighting in the friendly confines of Loftus Road in England, was still considered a heavy underdog. Certain groups in Ireland had criticized the fighter for marrying a Protestant and applying for British citizenship in order to advance his boxing career. The *Republican News*, the Sinn Fein-Provisional IRA newspaper, ran a headline, "Barry the Brit," castigating the fighter for pressing his own interests above those of his country. But McGuigan had always insisted that he was indeed fighting for the people of Ireland and not its politics. On the night of the Pedroza fight, he entered the ring bearing a neutral blue flag with a white dove of peace instead of either the tri-color or the Union Jack.

On this night, Ireland was united, and the scene at Loftus Road was every bit as electric as in pubs and gatherings across the British Isles. Following the Panamanian National Anthem, McGuigan's father Pat, a renowned Irish singer (also known by his stage name of Pat McGeehan), stepped into the ring and whipped the crowd into a frenzy with a passionate rendition of "Danny Boy." The moment echoed one of the most powerful themes of the song itself, a parent seeing his son off to battle. The younger McGuigan heard the call of the pipes, and beat Pedroza in a magnificent fight, bringing the title belt home to Clones.

A Catholic from the north of Ireland had united his fans, Catholic and Protestant, in song.

There are ancient angers and rancorous raging in the north of Ireland, with each side watching with painful sensitivity, lest the other side get any kind of cultural foothold. Song, therefore, is important. At football games (soccer to many of you), between teams from the north and the south, when the anthems have played "God Save the Queen" for the northerners and "The Soldiers Song" for the southerners, jeering and violence often erupt. "God Save the Queen" has been under intense scrutiny lately in Northern Ireland because the song celebrates the British State. In many of these discussions, "Danny Boy" is considered the favorite to replace it because it is considered "non-sectarian." So, it may be that when all these warring factions go to soccer games in the future, perhaps the melodious strains of the Derry air will soothe their agitated nerves. Maybe they will realize that it's just a game and not a bloody war which threatens all they hold dear. Why should anyone be surprised that "Danny Boy" has sparked debate in both the political and religious arenas? As recent as the summer of 2001, following the death of the beloved actor Carroll O'Connor (known to most as television's Archie Bunker), a funeral mass was held at St.

Paul the Apostle Catholic Church in Los Angeles, California, and over 1,000 friends and mourners turned out to pay their respects. Ending the ceremony, a violinist played a haunting rendition of "Danny Boy," and not long afterward, certain Dioceses of the Catholic church sent out word that no song deemed "secular" could be performed during funeral services, under any circumstances.

Naturally, this astounded me. What makes music sacred? The emotion it arouses in people? If they can, with a swift three-beat, transform bread and wine into the body and blood, can't a song be declared sacred? Perhaps this is just the "official" statement of these Dioceses. Several cities with large Irish populations have had Catholic churches suddenly go deaf when "Danny Boy" is either sung or played at funerals, despite their stance on secular music.

Irish American reaction has been fairly heated. Some have complained that most "sacred" music is elitist, whilst "Danny Boy" is a blue-collar song for the middle class. As a song of the people, just about everybody thinks it belongs to them. You can't attend a Catholic mass anymore without hearing "Amazing Grace" or "The Battle Hymn of the Republic." As if those aren't Protestant hymns! Perhaps the Catholic church would do well to reexamine the second verse, where Danny kneels and says "an Ave there for me." Then perhaps, a debate on the meaning of the word "secular" can begin in earnest.

It's comforting, then, to know that our boy Danny shows no sign of "sleeping in peace." In fact, he continues to wage new battles, despite the fact that the lyrics are nearly one hundred years old.

# Epilogue:
# In
# sunshine
# or in
# shadow

# What Does
# It All Mean?

$\mathcal{A}$ny spirit that has been touched by magnanimous love or overwhelming loss hears "Danny Boy" with an understanding that no amount of research or theorizing can illuminate completely. Music is, as Fred Weatherly so elegantly explained, perhaps the most powerful of all art forms, just as open to interpretation as works gracing the walls of the Guggenheim Museum. The rise and fall of a voice bidding Danny farewell evokes something quite different in each person. For one it may be the melancholy call of a mother to her son, and to another, the lament of a girl's love, lost to a land that promises wealth and freedom. The beauty of the song is held within the heart of the listener. We can only know the truth behind the melodic tune and the deceivingly simple lyrics by listening with our minds open and willing, free of myth or conjecture.

While "Danny Boy" will always be touted as an

Irish ballad, it was truly the product of many different worlds meshing together. Let it be the tune of a blind, Irish fiddler drifting across the sea, reaching an English barrister who would finally marry words and melody to create a song capable of describing, at least in part, the contents of the human heart. The song depicts the human condition, about the unknown and the black cloud of finality that accompanies it. The message is available to all those who want to hear it. "Danny Boy" has a profound effect on people from all corners of the world, a trait it shares with the truest of any work of art.

I have had the pleasure myself of meeting and speaking with some of the great Irish contemporary artists and performers in the world. I've always been curious about their reactions to "Danny Boy," the first time they heard the song or perhaps the most moving version they can recall.

Nobel Prize Winner Seamus Heaney is the poet responsible for penning breathtaking collections such as *Door into the Dark*, and *Preoccupations*, and the man some critics have described as "the most important Irish poet since Yeats." Born in Derry, the oldest of nine children, the song has special meaning to Heaney. Here he offers his own insightful analysis of "Danny Boy":

If you look at it on the page, the setting and the dramatic situation are conventional, the language full of romantic clichè. But your critical resistance soon fades when the singing begins. Very few people can hit the high notes at the end, but at the beginning I think nearly everybody can join in and feel they're in tune, so there's that community singing appeal. It's one of those songs, like "Shenandoa" and "The Water is Wide,"where the hankering in the music is as powerful as the hankering in the words, so you end up with this big, big waft of desire and nostalgia. Very simple devices work very effectively. You have the word pipes repeated straight away in the first line and that immediately creates the poignant mood which deepens when the note slows and lengthens itself out in the word "calling" and all of a sudden everything is even sadder. Next thing the summer's gone and the lover's being left alone and the sorrow is surging up and over us but no matter, we're all enjoying ourselves more than ever because it's so singable, the big ripples just keep widening out.

To Thomas Cahill, bestselling author of *How the Irish Saved Civilization*, the success of the song "Danny Boy" lies more in the melody, although the words are a beautiful evocation of loss. He feels that the song is the story of a woman bidding the man that she loves farewell as he departs during the time of The Great Hunger. She realizes that she will likely starve to death before he can send money to her to procure food, and she will have left this earth before he returns, having made his fortune.

Actor Liam Neeson will often sing the ballad to his sons, Mikey who is six and Danny who is five. In order to eschew the tiny battles that can erupt from the jealousy of young siblings, Liam will change the words, ever so slightly, not allowing the lyrics to show preference of one boy over the other. So fond of the song is he that he once requested that Barbara Streisand perform while they sat, riding in the same limousine. Unfortunately, his request was refused. Had it been Mr. Tom Waites riding along with him in that car, the disappointment may have been a bit greater, as it is Waites's rendition of the song that he most especially enjoys. But make no mistake, he will delight in almost any good, full-blown sentimental interpretation of the song. Wherever in the world he may travel and musicians be present he will ask that Danny Boy be played, sung or performed. Like most people, he does not know what the song means or what sad soul is having to say good bye to dear Danny, but it is of little concern to him, as it is one mystery that may remain unsolved as far as he's concerned.

The actress Roma Downey was raised in a working class area of Derry, the youngest of six children. As a Catholic, she was a minority in her hometown and often felt the sting of prejudice while negotiating the awkward stages of childhood. At the tender age of ten, Roma lost her mother to a sudden heart attack. As she grew she continued to be exposed to life's hardships. Her family bore witness to the horrific events of "Bloody Sunday," the name given to that fateful day when a civil rights match ended in the death of thirteen innocent people, some of whom she had known personally. Her father died before having the opportunity to see Roma graduate from college,yet another heartache she endured. And so, like most, it was not hard for her to feel the pangs of loss and longing summoned by this song

For actor, director, producer, and author Gabriel Byrne, it is Sinead O'Connor's version of the ballad, arranged by Sean Davies, that holds a special place in his heart. "It's a perfect song," he says, "and besides, Danny is

my father's name and I never hear it without being emotionally moved and remembering not alone my father but
the history that stretches behind him."

My brother, Frank McCourt, author of *Angela's
Ashes* and *'Tis*, became quite familiar with the tune and
words, growing up in Limerick. At any concert in town,
'twas certain that at least one singer would have a go at
"Danny Boy." Women cried, he remembered, and men got
misty eyed. Tears that were somehow understood by all.

Frank believes "Danny Boy" to be a song of an
emigrant with only a vestige of hope of a happy return.
The Irish man who left the Emerald Isle behind was rarely
seen again trekking across his native soil. And so the sadness of final goodbyes is woven quite clearly into the
lyrics. One fall day, Frank walked along the streets of
Brooklyn with his friend Herbert Miller. He remarked
"the summer's gone and all the flowers are dying." Miller
turned to him, his face contorted in a grimace. Aghast,
Miller declared, "that is a dreadful thing to say." Frank's
explanation that he was simply quoting the words to a
famous song seemed to have fallen on deaf ears.

And so, from glen to glen, we've finally come to
the end of our journey. If you've made it this far, there's
no need to sum up the bittersweet emotions embodied in

the song. I believe we can concur on that point. And, of course, you must be aware that a proper sendoff is certainly in order here.

So, once more, all together:

*Oh, Danny boy, the pipes, the pipes are calling*
*From glen to glen and down the mountain side*
*The summer's gone and all the flowers are dying*
*It's you, it's you must go and I must bide.*

*But come ye back when summer's in the meadow*
*Or when the valley's hushed and white with snow*
*It's I'll be there in sunshine or in shadow*
*Oh, Danny boy, oh Danny boy, I love you so!*

*And if ye come, and all the flow'rs are dying*
*If I am dead, as dead I well may be*
*Ye'll come and find the place where I am lying*
*And kneel and say an Ave there for me.*

*And I shall hear, though soft you tread above me*
*And all my grave will warmer, sweeter be*
*For you will bend and tell me that you love me*
*And I shall sleep in peace until you come to me.*

# Appendix

# Discography
and Time Line

# THE INCOMPLETE
# DISCOGRAPHY

*I*t would be a cumbersome task to list every rendition of "Danny Boy" ever recorded because so many artists have performed the song over the years. Freddie Mercury of Queen used to sing it in the 1970s to exuberant crowds whenever the band toured Ireland. Sinead O'Connor did a version of the ballad that was arranged by Sean Davies and Eric Clapton performed a breathtaking instrumental rendition. Movies have even been known to turn to "Danny Boy" to help deliver an emotionally touching moment from time to time. *Brassed Off* and *Family Business* are two such films.

Elvis Presley liked to sing the song leisurely, but struggled with the high notes and never attempted a recording. But toward the very end of his career, RCA arranged to record Elvis, and after ten takes and singing in a lower key, the King finally produced a version he was happy with. The song was included on the 1976 album, "From Elvis Presley Boulevard, Memphis, Tennessee."

# Danny Boy Discography

*Odyssey Of Paul Robeson*
Paul Robeson
Vanguard Classics

*Kate Smith*
Kate Smith
BMG

*Golden Greats*
Glenn Miller
BMG

*Volume 1, Songs of Old Ireland*
Melody Greenwood
PMF Records

*Golden Celebration—Elvis 50th*
Elvis Presley
BMG/RCA

*Off To Philadelphia*
Frances Lucey
Amati

*Best of Ireland*
Bing Crosby
Madacy Records

*Irish Dance*
Va-celtic Pride
Riverdance

*Requestfully Yours*
Flamingos
Westside (UK)  DNA

*It's Only Make Believe*
Conway Twitty
Music Club

*Live at Harrah's*
Glenn Yarborough
Folk Era

*Shine On*
Riot
Metal Blade

*Our Point Of View*
New Coon Creek Girls
Pinecastle

*Best of Lonely Guitar*
Duane Eddy
One Way Records

*This Is Jazz No. 33*
Tony Bennett
Sony/Columbia

*The Toast*
Memphis Belle
Modine, Stoltz, Donovan, Sweeney
Warner Studios

*Tom Jones*
Tom Jones
Gold Sound (Italy)

*1946–1947*
Count & His Orchestra Basie
Jazz Chronological Classics

"Danny Boy"
Rufus Wainwright
Uni/Dream Works Records

*A & E Biography*
Judy Garland
EMD/Capitol

*Super Sellers of The 50's*
Conway Twitty
Super Doubles

*The Sea of Dreams*
Davy Spillane-featuring Sinead O'Connor
Covert

"Concord Jazz Heritage Series"
Herb Ellis
Concord Jazz

"Danny Boy–1955"
Memories Of You
Rosemary Clooney

"Le Mor Ghra—with Lots Of Love"
Jimmy O'byrne
Rego Irish

"I Remember You"
Ben Wilmot
Orchard

"Hush Hush Sweet Charlotte/Gentle on My Mind"
Patti Page
Collectables Records

*Ireland's Greatest Love Songs*
Josef Locke
Sounds Of Ireland (UK)

"He's So Fine/Lonely Teardrops"
Jackie Wilson
Diablo (UK)

"Titan Of Soul"
Jackie Wilson
Demon Duplicate Numbers (UK)

*Judy*
Judy Garland
32 Records


"London Donnie (Danny Boy)"
*1946*
Don Byas
Jazz Chronological Classics


*Greatest Hits*
Jackie Wilson
Brunswick


"Londonderry Aire (Danny Boy)"
*Celtic Harpestry*
Deborah Henson-Conant
Uni/Imaginary Road


"In the Mood"
Glenn Miller
Cleopatra


*Ireland in Song*
Frank Patterson
BMG/RCA Victor

*Live at the Apollo*
Patti & Blue Belles Labelle
Blue Moon (UK)

*Best of Early Years*
Patti & Blue Belles Labelle
Uni/Hip-o Records

*Irish Melodies*
Leo Mccaffrey
Compose

"Tears of Stone"
Chieftains
BMG/RCA Victor

*In the Glenn Miller Mood*
Airmen Of Note
Altissimo

"Best of Bronn Journey"
Bronn Journey
Revere

*Love Songs & Ballads*
Tom Jones
32 Jazz Records

"Down by the Glenside"
Sheila Ryan
Orchard

"Lucky"
Terry Clarke
Appaloosa

*Ultimate Collection*
Mario Lanza
MSI

"You Take My Breath Away" (with Danny Boy)
*Danny's Island*
Danny Lerman
Chartmaker

*Greatest Hits*
J.J. Sheridan
Trigon

*Vol. 2—in The Vaults*
Ventures
Ace (UK)

"Double Duke"
Joe Temperley
Naxos Jazz

"Day-O"
Harry Belafonte
MSI"

"Come By Me"
Harry Connick Jr.
Sony/Columbia

*Irish Standards*
Roger Whittaker
BMG Special Products

*Great Irish Tenors*
Robert White
BMG/RCA Victor

*British & Irish Pub Songs*
Paddy Band Macnamara
Goldies

"Medley-Sugar Sugar/Everything Is Beautiful/
Bridge Over Troubled Water/Danny Boy"
*Neil Sedaka Sings The Hits*
Neil Sedaka
BMG/RCA

"Time Remembered"
Bill Evans Trio
Fantasy/Milestone

*Irish Celebration*
Paddy Noonan
Compose

*America's Favorite Irish Tenor*
Dennis Day
Star Line I

"Here's to the Irish"
Leo McCaffrey
Madacy Records

"Celtic Tranquility"
Phil Coulter
Erin

"It Might as Well be the Moon"
Mickey Newbury
Mountain Retreat

*Legend at His Best*
Al Hirt
Collectables Records

"Londonderry Air (Danny Boy) Magic Of Celtic Harp"
Claire Hamilton
Premium Music Collection

*California Sun—Best of the Rivieras*
Rivieras
Norton

"Barbar's Lament"
Eddie Dillon
Orchard

"Moody Blue"
Elvis Presley
BMG/RCA

*Decca Years 1962–72*
Bachelors
Pid

"Danny Boy"
John McDermott
MSI

"Unsung Blues Legend"
Lonnie Johnson
Blues Magnet

"Memories Are Made of This"
Ruby Murray
PID

*Classic Ballads*
Tom Jones
PID

"Heart to Heart"
Betty Buckley
KO Productions

*Live at Wolf Trap*
Judy Collins
Wildflower

*Songs I Love to Play*
Johnny Carroll
Our Heritage

"Counting Teardrops"
Emile Ford
Castle Music America

"Empathy/Simple Matter"
Bill Evans
Uni/Verve

*16 Biggest Hits*
Ray Price
Sony/Epic

"Ellis Island"
Irish Tenors
Music Matters

*You'll Never Walk Alone*
Original Blind Boys Of Alabama
Collectables Records

*Andy Williams Live*
Andy Williams
Concord/Neon Tonic

*Golden Years: 1938–42*
Glenn Miller
Proper Records

"Windflower"
Herb Ellis
Concord Jazz

"In New York City"
Scott Hamilton
Concord Jazz

"Demi Centennial"
Rosemary Clooney
Concord Jazz

"Ballad for Americans"
Paul Robeson
Vanguard

*Best of Boxcar Willie*
Boxcar Willie
Madacy Records

*Man In Black 1963–69*
Johnny Cash
Bear Family Records

"Welcome to My World"
Jim Reeves
Bear Family

"Please Help Me I'm Falling"
Hank Locklin
Bear Family Records

*Rose Marie—His Recordings 1949*
Slim Whitman
Bear Family Records

*Locust Years... And the Return to the Promised Land*
Jerry Lee Lewis
Bear Family Records

*Kissin, Twistin, Goin, Where the Boys Are*
Connie Francis
Bear Family Records

*Honky Tonk Years 1950–66*
Ray Price & the Cherokee Cowboys
Bear Family Records

"Irish Nightingale"
Morton Downey
Asv Living Era

"Dream of Erin"
Timmy Flaherty
Hot Records

*20 Greatest Hits*
Johnny Paycheck
Deluxe

*Great Mahalia Jackson*
Mahalia Jackson
Sony/Columbia

*16 Most Requested Songs*
Andy Williams
Sony/Columbia

*Global Masters*
Johnny Mathis
Sony/Columbia

"Diamonds & Rust"
Joan Baez
Uni/A & M

*Papa John Creach*
Papa John Creach
One Way Records

"My Romance"
Carly Simon
BMG/Arista

*From Elvis Presley Boulevard, Memphis, Tennessee*
Elvis Presley
BMG/RCA

*Home of the Brave*
Black 47

*My Favorite Irish Songs*
Bing Crosby
MCA

"Voice of an Angel"
Charlotte Church
Sony Classics

# TIMELINE

**6000 B.C..** The first human settlements in Ireland.

**600–150 B.C.** Gaels from western Europe invaded Ireland and subdued the previous inhabitants.

**250 B.C.** Laigin from Armorica in northwestern France arrived in southeast Ireland.

**50 A.D.** Gaeil or Goidets migrate from Europe to the Kenmare River in south Kerry and the Boyne estuary near Drogheda.

**600** St. Brendan of Kerry is said to have sailed to North America (not proven).

**795** Vikings land near St. Columcille's monastery on Lambay Island.

**800–850** Norwegian Vikings plunder many Irish monasteries. In 845, Thorgils, king of the Norsemen in Ireland, is captured and killed by Maelseachlainn, king of Meath.

**853** Danish fleet defeats the Norwegians and takes possession of Dublin.

**1507** Accession of Henry VIII.

**1515** Anarchy in Ireland.

**1534** Kildare rebellion.

**1547–1549** Henry VIII made his great breach with Rome, and set himself up as the head of the Church of England.

**1548** Henry VIII declares himself king of Ireland.

**1548** Henry VIII dies and is succeeded by the boy king Edward VI.

**1577** Mary ascends the throne.

**1558** Accession of Elizabeth I.

**1577** Elizabethan wars in Ireland.

**1577** Spanish Armada sent by Phillip of Spain to conquer England.

**1594** Accession of James I. Surrender of Hugh O'Neill. Enforcement of English Law in Ireland.

**1595** Rebellion of Hugh O'Neill, Earl of Tyrone.

**1601** Defeat of O'Neill, O'Donnell and Spaniards by Mountjoy at Battle of Kinsale.

**1632–38** Compilation of the Annals of the Four Masters.

**1641** Great Catholic-Gaelic rebellion for return of lands, later joined by Old English Catholic in Ireland. Under leadership of Irish chieftain, Rory O'Moore, conspiracy was formed to seize Dublin and expel the English. English settlers were driven out of Ulster. Catholics hold 59% of land in Ireland.

**1642** Confederation of Kilkenny met.

**1647** Alliance between lords of Pale and native Irishmen came to an end.

**1648** English soldier and statesman, Oliver Cromwell, landed at Dublin. His troops killed 2,000 men. A great part of lands in Munster, Leinster and Ulster (Drogheda and Wexford) were confiscated and divided among the English soldiers.

**1651** The Siege of Limerick.

**1656** Over 60,000 Irish Catholics had been sent as slaves to Barbados and other islands in the Caribbean.

**1658** The population of Ireland, estimated at 1,500,000 before Cromwell, was reduced by two-thirds, to 500,000, at his death in 1658.

**1659** The Siege of Derry.

**1660** Accession of Charles II.

**1661–68** The Duke of Ormond ruled Ireland as Viceroy.

**1672** Over 6,000 Irish boys and women sold as slaves since England gained control of Jamaica.

**1685** Rory Dall O'Cahan (aka Rory Dall Morrison and Rory Dall, 1660-1712), an Irish harper, may have composed the melody later known as the Londonderry air. Accession of James II.

**1688** Protestant Apprentice Boys close gates, raise drawbridge and refuse to surrender to Catholic forces in Derry; James II's Parliament restored all lands confiscated since 1641. Catholics now hold 22% of land in Ireland.

**1689** William of Orange lands at Carrickfergus and defeats James II at Battle of the Boyne.

**1690** Catholic defeat at Aughrim and surrender at Limerick.

**1692–1829** Exclusion of Catholics from Parliament and all professions.

**1695** Anti-Catholic Penal Laws introduced. Catholics hold 14% of land in Ireland.

**1698** William Molyneaux pamphlet against England making laws for Irelend.

**Early 1700s** Ancient Scottish manuscript originating from Lowland Scotland appears to include a melody very similar to the melody of the Londonderry air.

**1714** Catholics hold 7% of land in Ireland.

**1740** The Forgotten Famine.

**1770** Thomas Moore is born.

**1775** Henry Grattan becomes leader of the Patriot Party; Daniel O'Connell born at Derrynane, County Kerry. He received early schooling from Parish Priest and was then sent to France to receive further instruction at St. Omer and Douai.

**1782** Legislative Independence won from Britain by Irish Parliament.

**1789** George Petrie is born.

**1798** Act of Union passed.

**1803** Robert Emmett's rising, trial and execution.

**1823** Daniel O'Connell's Catholic Association founded.

**1828** Catholic emancipation passed; Tithe war began.

**1831** James Hardiman publishes Irish Minstrelry, which includes "Aisling an Oigfhir" which is strikingly similar to what would later be known as the Londonderry air.

**1834** Thomas Moore publishes a ten-volume work, *Irish Melodies*, with one poem, "My Gentle Harp," set to a melody which may have been an earlier version of the Londonderry air.

**1837** Accession of Queen Victoria.

**1838** O'Connell's Repeal Association founded.

**1842** *The Nation* newspaper founded by Thomas Davis.

**1843** Blight in the Potato Harvest.

**1845–1849** Beginning of Famine; Charles Treveleyan, permanent head of Treasury. Sir Robert Peel, Prime Minister, imports Indian corn.

**1846** Lord John Russell replaces Peel as Prime Minister.

**1848** Fever spreading. Treveleyan winds up Soup Kitchen Act, and retires to write history of famine

**1849** Frederick Edward Weatherly is born in Portishead, England.

**1848** Smith O'Brien (Young Ireland Leader) arrested. James Stephens flees to France.

**1848–49** Worst years of famine; by 1848 through emigration and deaths by famine, Ireland's population decreased by more than 2 million people.

**1851** Blind fiddler Jimmy McCurry plays frequently on Maine Street during fair days at the Limavady market.

**1851** Miss Jane Ross of Limavady County Derry annotates an air she heard played by an itinerant piper (possibly Jimmy McCurry) along Maine Street, where her house is.

**1852** Thomas Moore dies.

**1855** Dr. George Petrie publishes *Ancient Music of Ireland*, crediting Miss Jane Ross for annotating the Londonderry air.

**1856** Stephens returns from France.

**1857** Stephens founds Irish Republican Brotherhood. Fenian Brotherhood founded in America.

**1861** Beginning of American Civil War.

**1863** *Irish People* newspaper founded.

**1865** End of American Civil War. Arrest of editorial board of *Irish People*. James Stephens arrested and escapes from Richmond Jail.

**1866** Dr. George Petrie dies.

**1867** Abortive raid on Chester Castle. Fenian rising in Ireland. Clerkenwell explosion.

**1869** Gladstone, Prime Minister, dis-establishes Protestant Church in Ireland.

1877 Weatherly receives his call to the Bar at the Inner Temple, taking chambers with Henry Dickens, son of the eminent novelist.

1879 Threat of famine. Evictions. Irish National League founded.

1879–82 Land War.

1881 Gladstone's 2nd Land Act. Parnell imprisoned.

1882 Kilmainham "Treaty." Parnell's release. Phoenix Park Murders.

1886 First Home Rule Bill.

1891 Parnell loses three by-elections in Ireland. Parnell dies in October.

1893 Weatherly joins the Local Bar in Bristol, beginning a very successful law practice. Second Home Rule Bill. Gaelic League formed.

1903 Land Purchase Act (Wyndham Act).

**1910** Frederick E. Weatherly writes the lyrics to "Danny Boy" for another melody.

**1912** Frederick E. Weatherly receives the Londonderry air from a sister-in-law in America. Weatherly likes the tune and slightly reworks "Danny Boy" to fit the air.

**1913** "Danny Boy" is published by Boosey and Hawkes in London.

**1914** World War I breaks out in Europe.

**1916** Weatherly writes "Roses of Picardy," a very popular song of the time.

**1918** Sinn Fein wins a majority of Irish seats in Westminster parliament elections.

**1926** G.P. Putnam's Sons publishes Weatherly's autobiography, *Piano and Gown*.

**1929** Weatherly dies, leaving behind a collection of more than 1,500 published verses.

**1932** General Election. Fianna Fail victory.

**1937** Constitution of "Eire"claims 32 counties.

**1939** Second World War.

**1945** End of Second World War.

**1948** General Election. Fianna Fail defeated.

**1949** External Relations Act. Ireland leaves Commonwealth. Republic of Ireland declared (26 counties).

**1951-62** IRA campaign in North.

**1955** Ireland joins the United Nations.

**1965** O'Neill-Lemass Talks.

**1967** Northern Ireland Civil Rights Association founded.

**1968** First Civil Rights March. Derry Civil Rights March, banned by William Craig, Minister of Home Affairs, held but broken up by police brutality.

**1969** People's Democracy Belfast to Derry Civil Rights March. Marchers attacked at Burntollet Bridge. O'Neill resigns. Chichester Clark named Prime Minister. British troops sent to Derry. Protestant riot in Belfast.

**1970** Dublin Arms Trial.

**1972** January 30: Bloody Sunday in Derry. British paratroopers shoot 13 civilians during civil-rights march. Stormont suspended.

**1973** Sunningdale agreement.

**1974** Ulster workers strike brings down Faulkner and assembly. Direct Rule re-imposed. Loyalists bomb Dublin and Monaghan, killing 30.

**1981-82** Ten republicans die on hunger strike in Maze Prison.

**1985** Anglo-Irish Agreement signed.

**1994** Peace Declaration and IRA cease-fire.

**1996** Cease-fire breaks down after Britain's Conservative government refuses to allow Sinn Fein to join all-party talks on NI.

**1997** IRA cease-fire resumes; talks begin in Belfast between government of Irish Republic, Britain's new labor government, and representatives of all NI's political parties.

**1998** Initial peace-plan accepted by all parties.